THE HEART

Alan Trussell-Cullen

NELSON
CENGAGE Learning

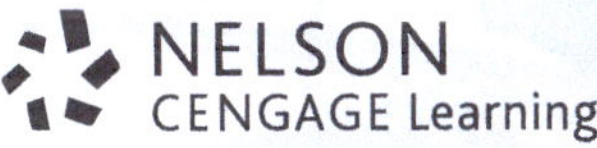

Australia • Brazil • Japan • Korea • Mexico • Singapore • Spain • United Kingdom • United States

The Heart

Fast Forward
Green Level 14

Text: Alan Trussell-Cullen
Illustrations: Stuart Billington and Melissa Webb
Editor: Johanna Rohan
Design: Vonda Pestana
Series design: James Lowe
Production controller: Emma Hayes
Photo research: Johanna Rohan and Gillian Cardinal
Audio recordings: Juliet Hill, Picture Start
Spoken by: Matthew King and Abbe Holmes

Acknowledgements
The author and publisher would like to acknowledge permission to reproduce material from the following sources:

Photographs by Getty Images/PhotoDisc, cover, pp 12, 23/ 3D Clinic, pp 4, 20 right/ Iconica, p 5/ Stone, pp 6 top, 18 right/ Taxi, pp 7 top, 18 left/ The Image Bank, pp 17, 21 top/ Asia Images, p 20 left; istockphoto, p 7 bottom; Masterfile/Tim Kiusalaas, p 21 bottom; Photolibrary.com/Foodpix, p 10/ Photonica, p 19.

ISBN 978 0 17 012590 1
ISBN 978 0 17 012585 7 (set)

Cengage Learning Australia
Level 7, 80 Dorcas Street
South Melbourne, Victoria Australia 3205
Phone: 1300 790 853

Cengage Learning New Zealand
Unit 4B Rosedale Office Park
331 Rosedale Road, Albany, North Shore NZ 0632
Phone: 0800 449 725

For learning solutions, visit **cengage.com.au**

Printed in Australia by Ligare Pty Ltd
11 12 13 14 15 16 17 19 18 17 16 15

Evaluated in independent research by staff from the Department of Language, Literacy and Arts Education at the University of Melbourne.

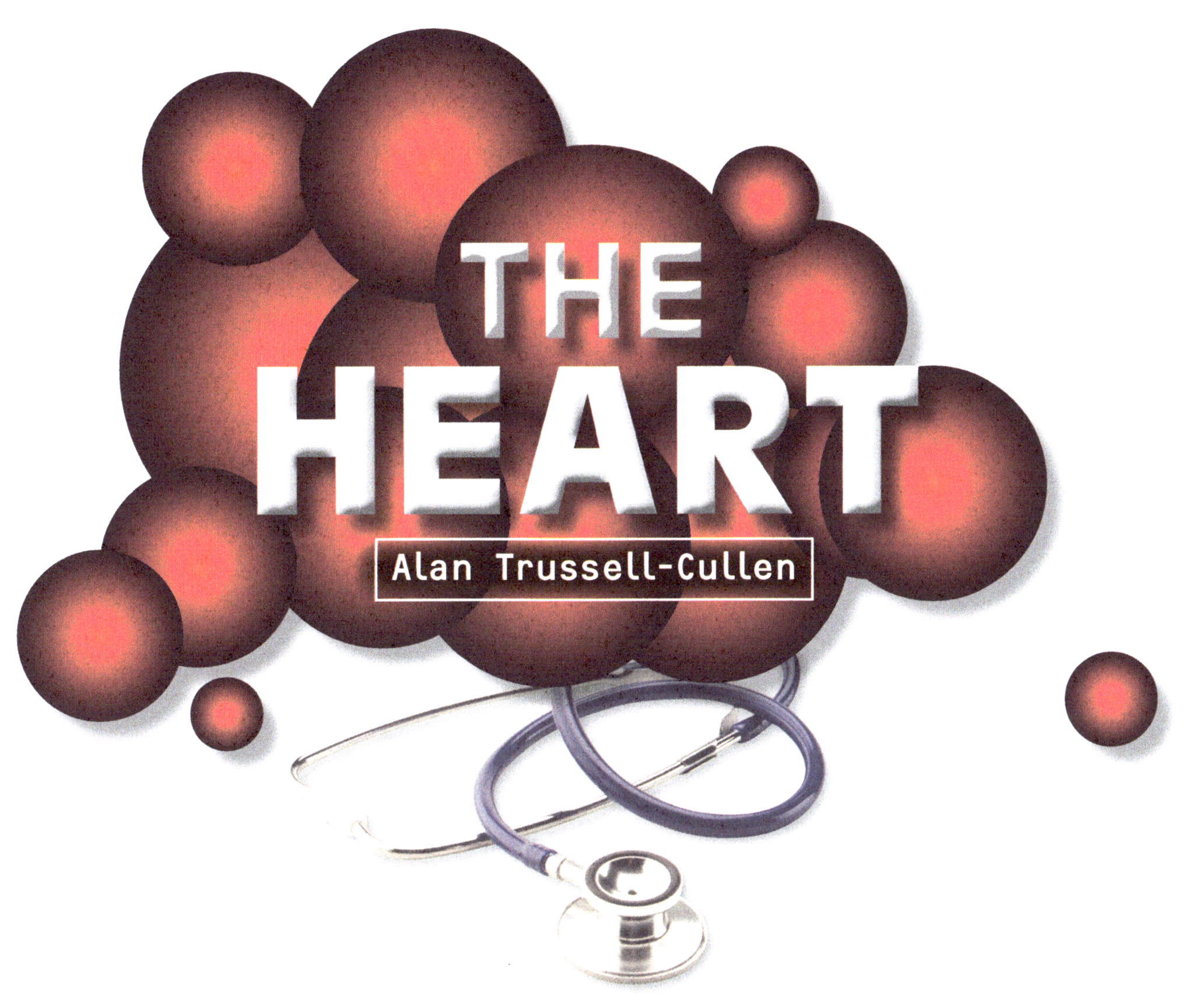

Contents

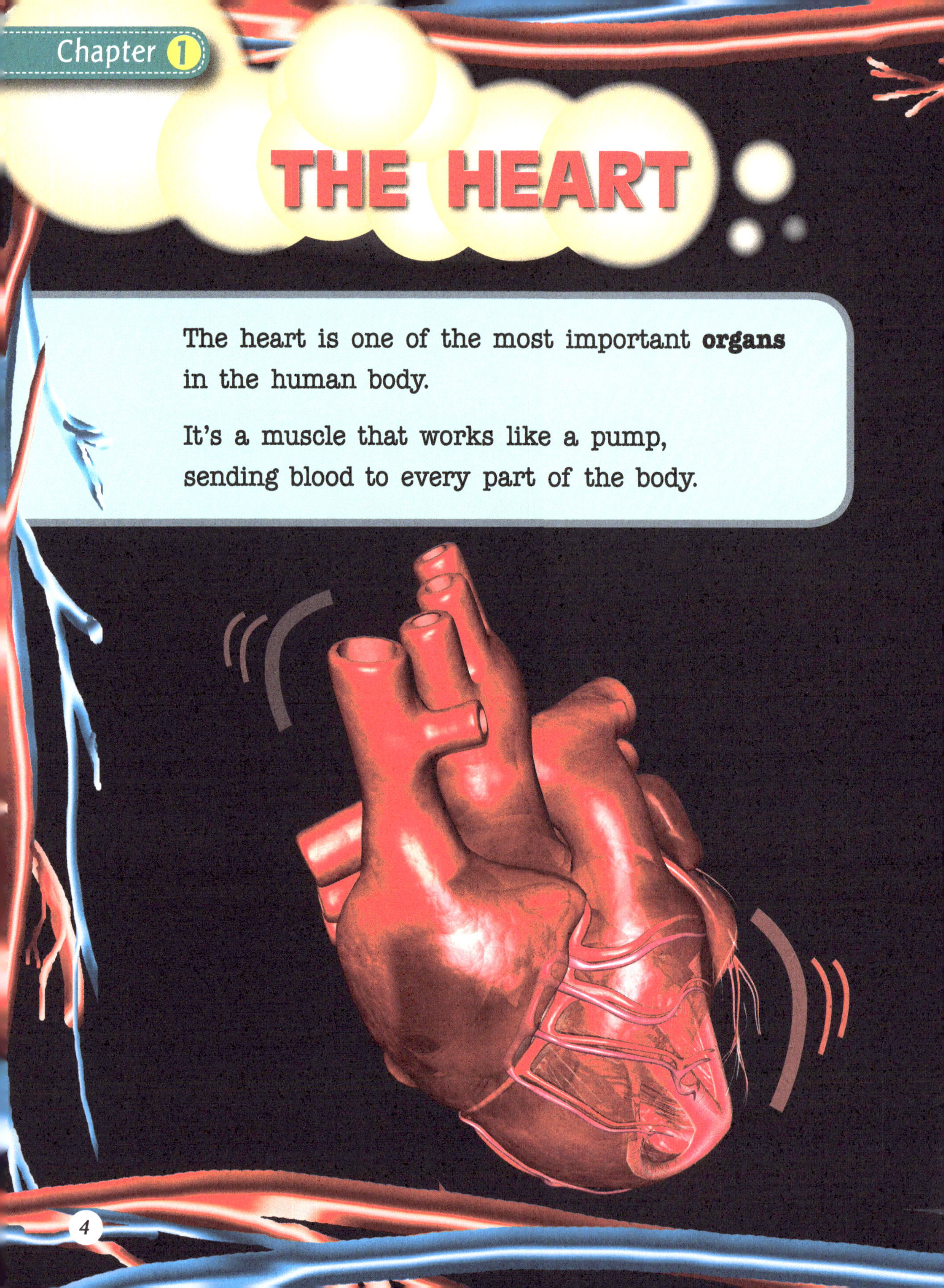

Chapter 1

THE HEART

The heart is one of the most important **organs** in the human body.

It's a muscle that works like a pump, sending blood to every part of the body.

The body needs this blood to stay alive.

It takes 20 seconds for the heart to pump blood to every **cell** in the body.

Chapter 2

WHAT THE HEART LOOKS LIKE

The heart can be found
in the middle of the chest,
behind the ribs.
The ribs help to keep the heart safe.

A child's heart is about the size of a fist.
An adult's heart is about the size of two fists.

A blue whale's heart is about as big as a small car.

The heart has four places that hold blood.

It has two large places on the bottom.
These are called the right ventricle and left ventricle.

It has two smaller places on the top.
These are called the right atrium and left atrium.

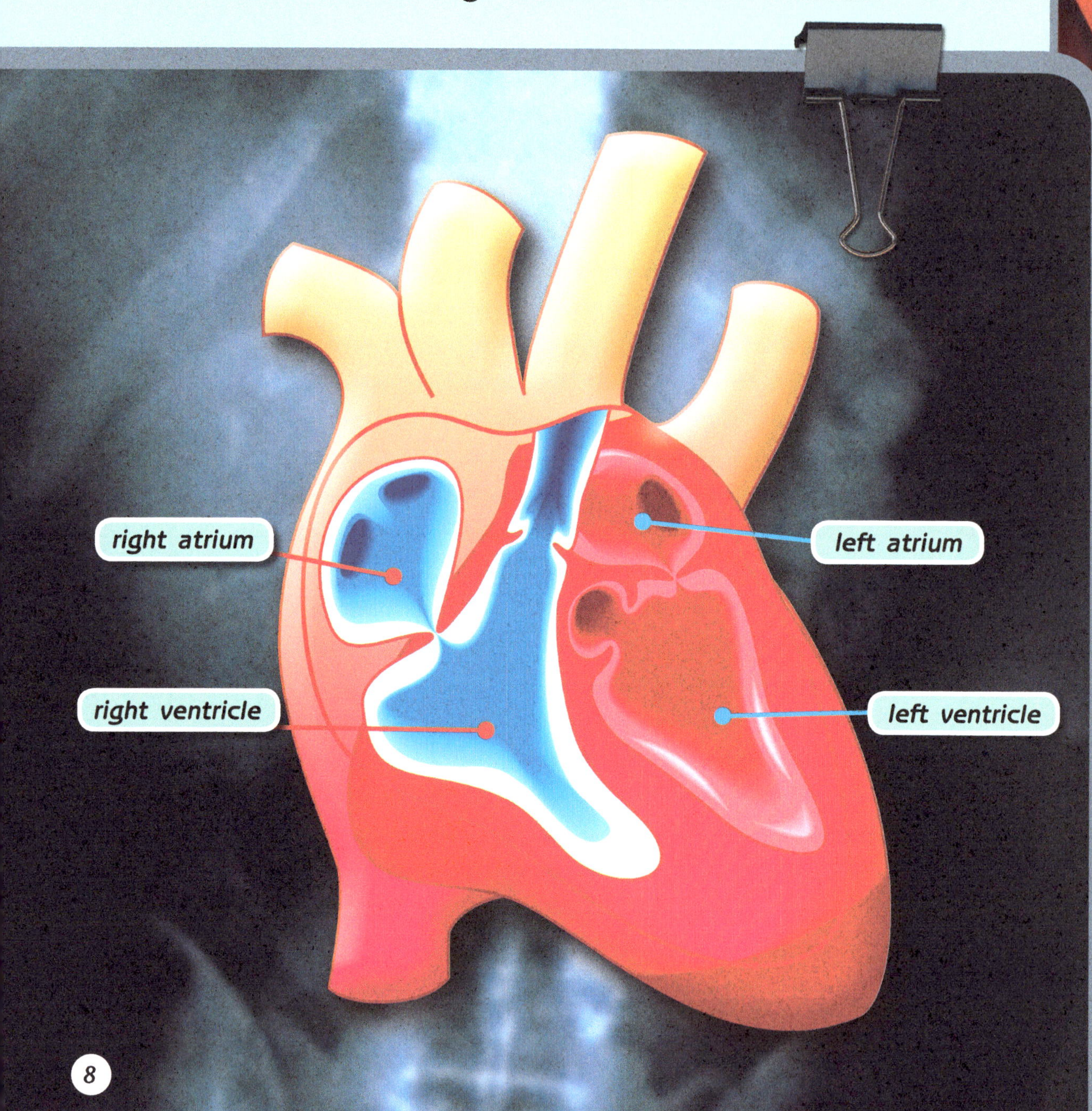

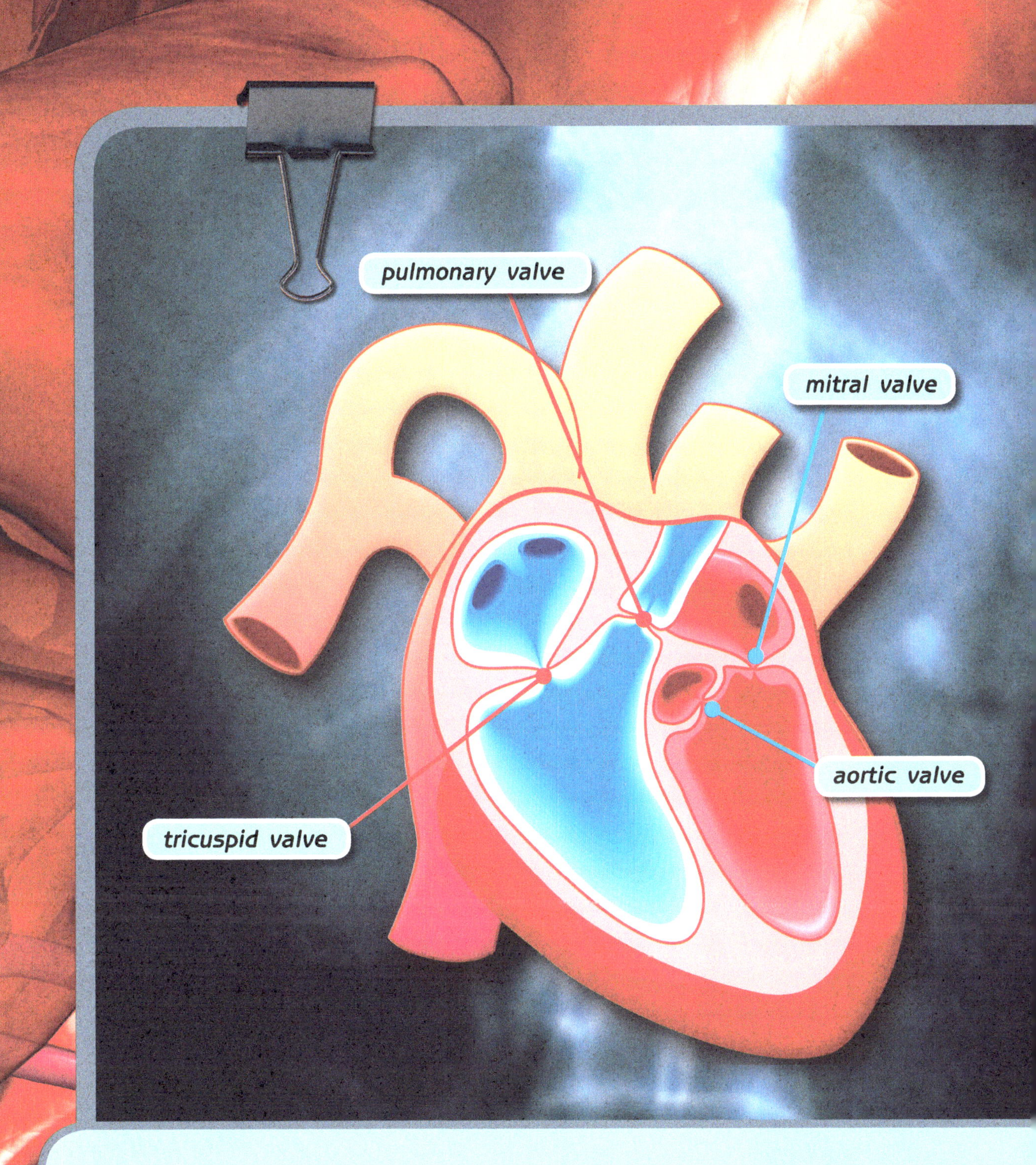

There are four **valves** in the heart.
The valves stop the blood going back the wrong way.

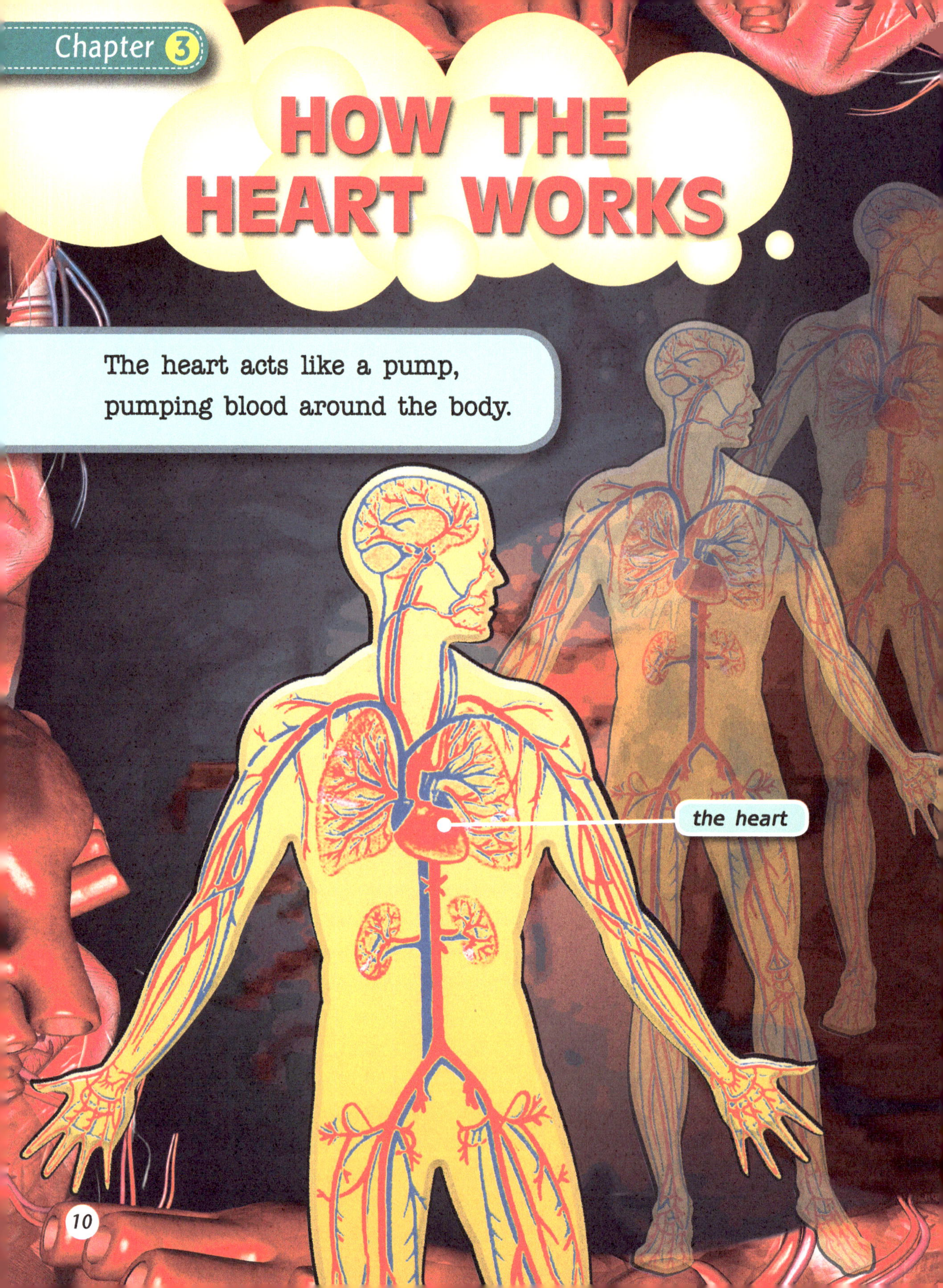

Chapter 3

HOW THE HEART WORKS

The heart acts like a pump, pumping blood around the body.

The blood takes important things like oxygen and food to every part of the body.
Without oxygen and food,
the body's cells begin to die.
The blood also takes away things
the body doesn't need.

Running Words 184

About 8 million blood cells die every second. The same number of blood cells are born every second.

After the blood has been pumped around the body, it comes back to the heart.

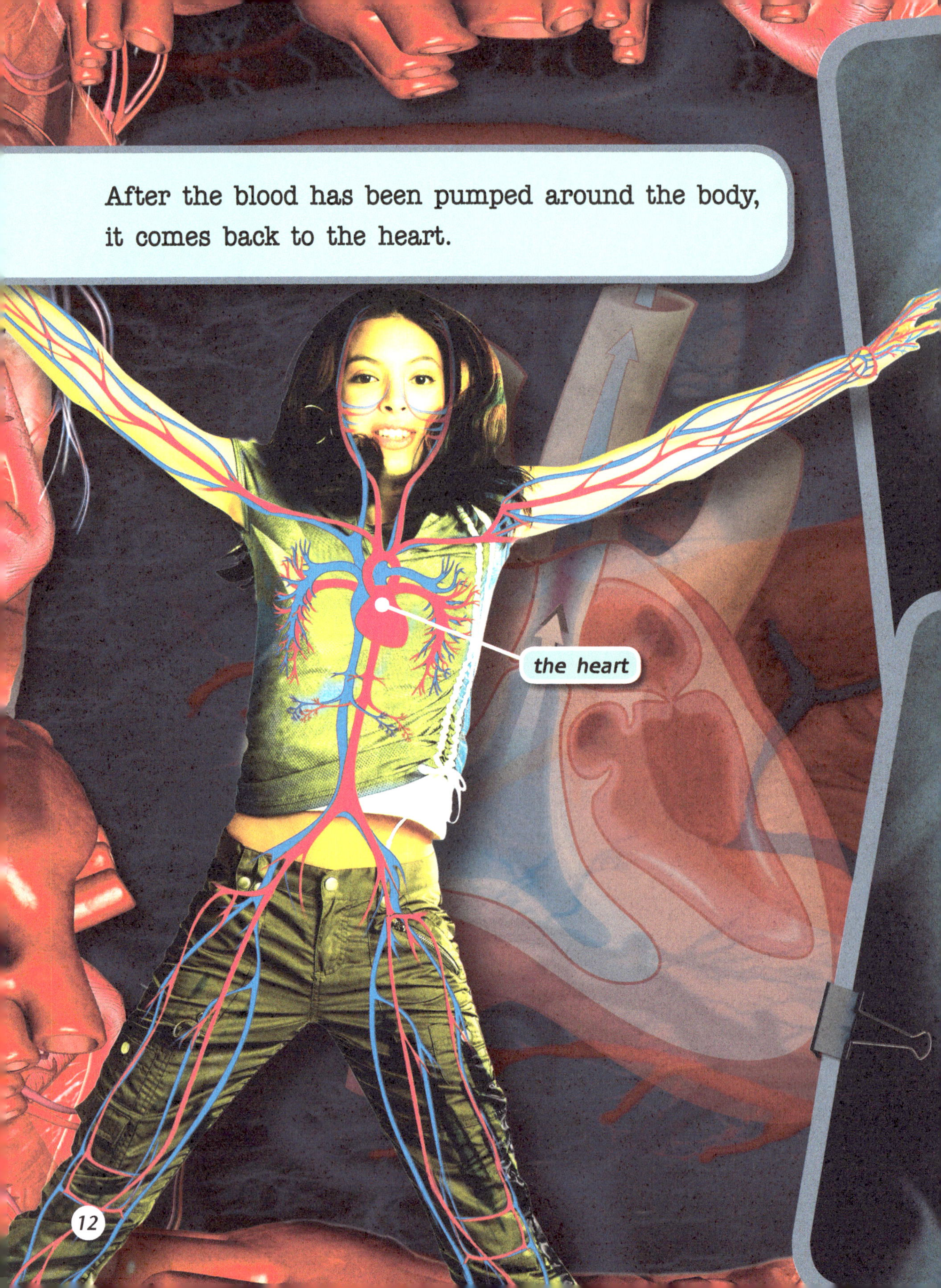

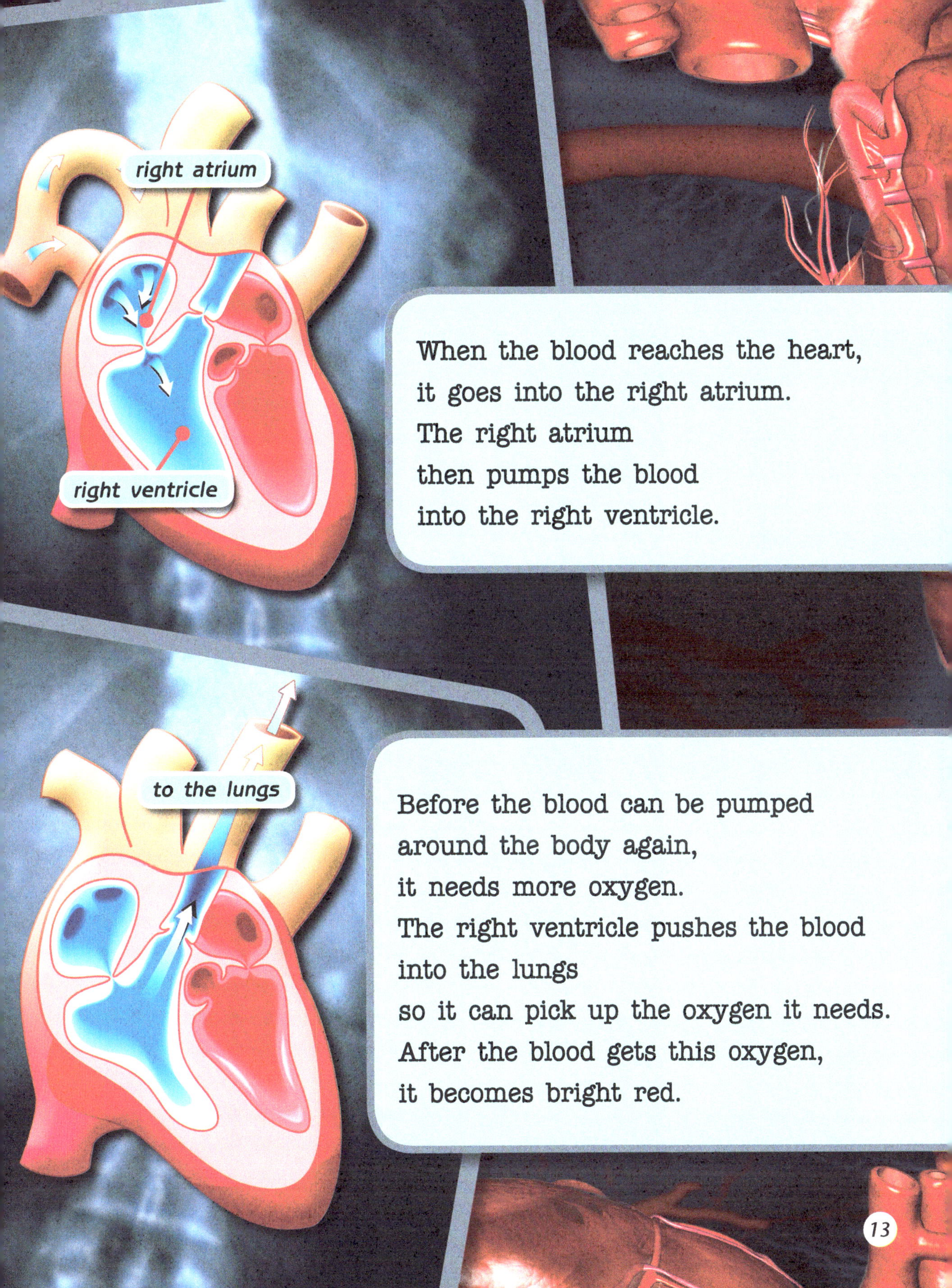

When the blood reaches the heart,
it goes into the right atrium.
The right atrium
then pumps the blood
into the right ventricle.

Before the blood can be pumped
around the body again,
it needs more oxygen.
The right ventricle pushes the blood
into the lungs
so it can pick up the oxygen it needs.
After the blood gets this oxygen,
it becomes bright red.

When the blood leaves the lungs, it goes back to the left atrium.

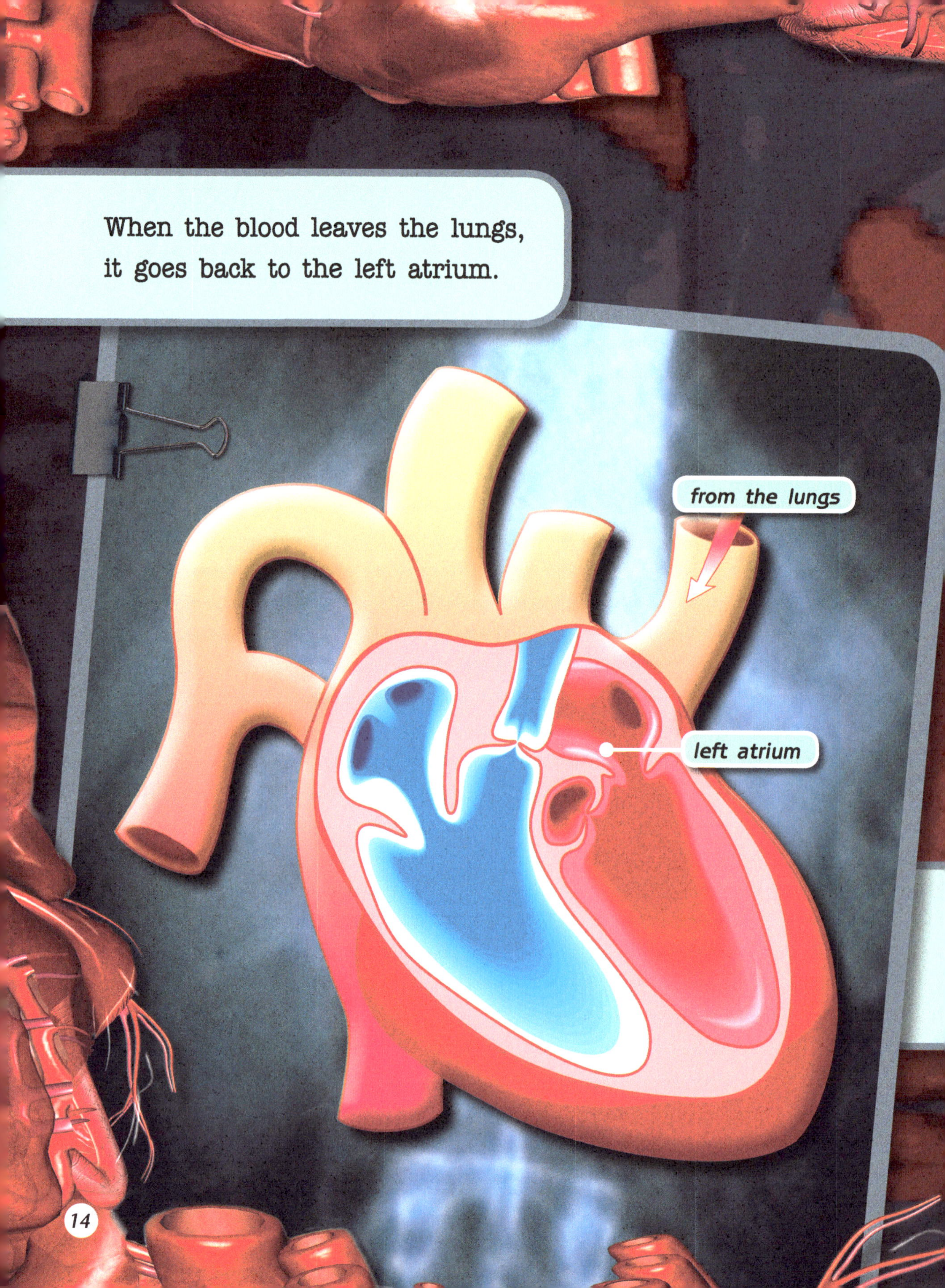

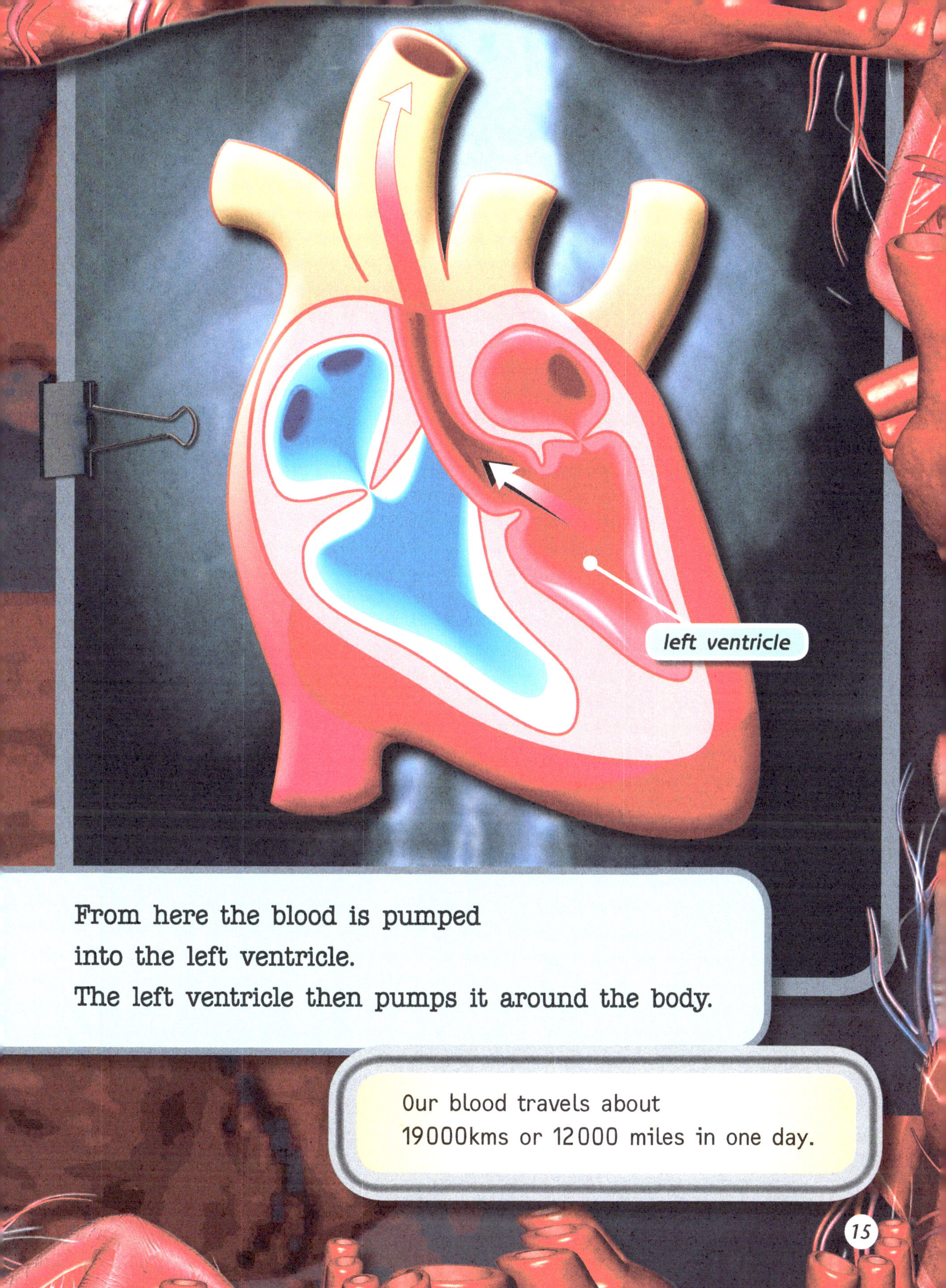

From here the blood is pumped
into the left ventricle.
The left ventricle then pumps it around the body.

Our blood travels about
19000kms or 12000 miles in one day.

THE BEATING HEART

The beating sound of the heart is made by the four valves inside the heart.

A beating sound is made each time a valve closes to stop blood going the wrong way.

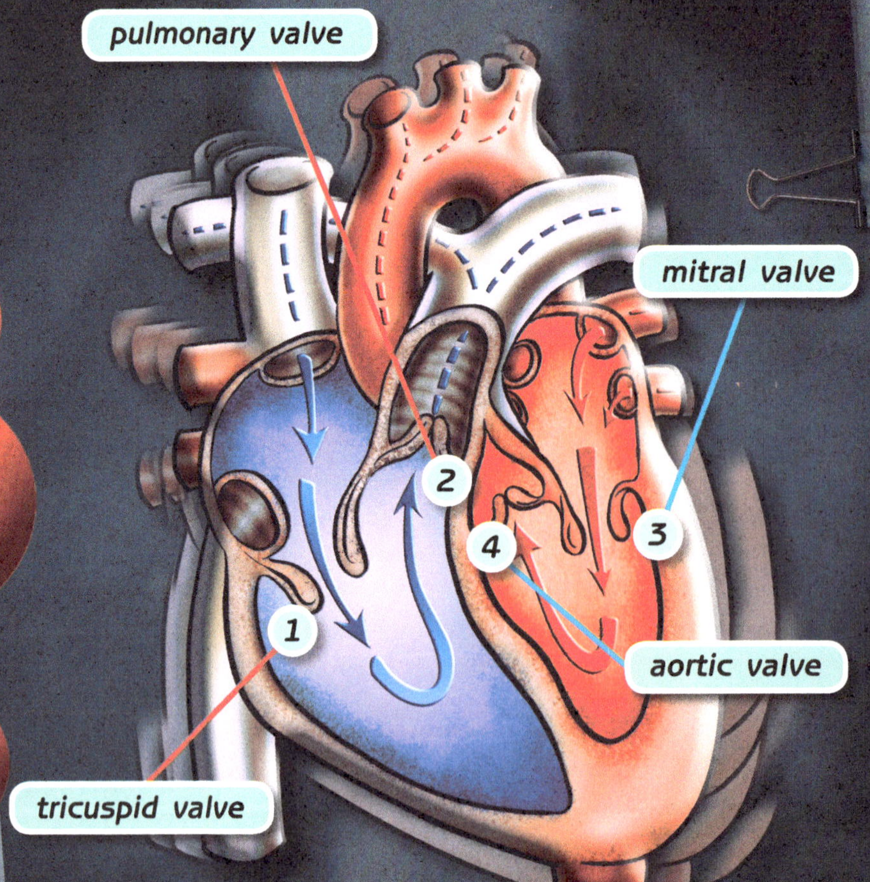

the four valves

There are many ways to listen to someone's heart beat.

Before each heart beat,
the heart fills with blood,
then it pushes the blood out.

The heart does this all day
and all night.

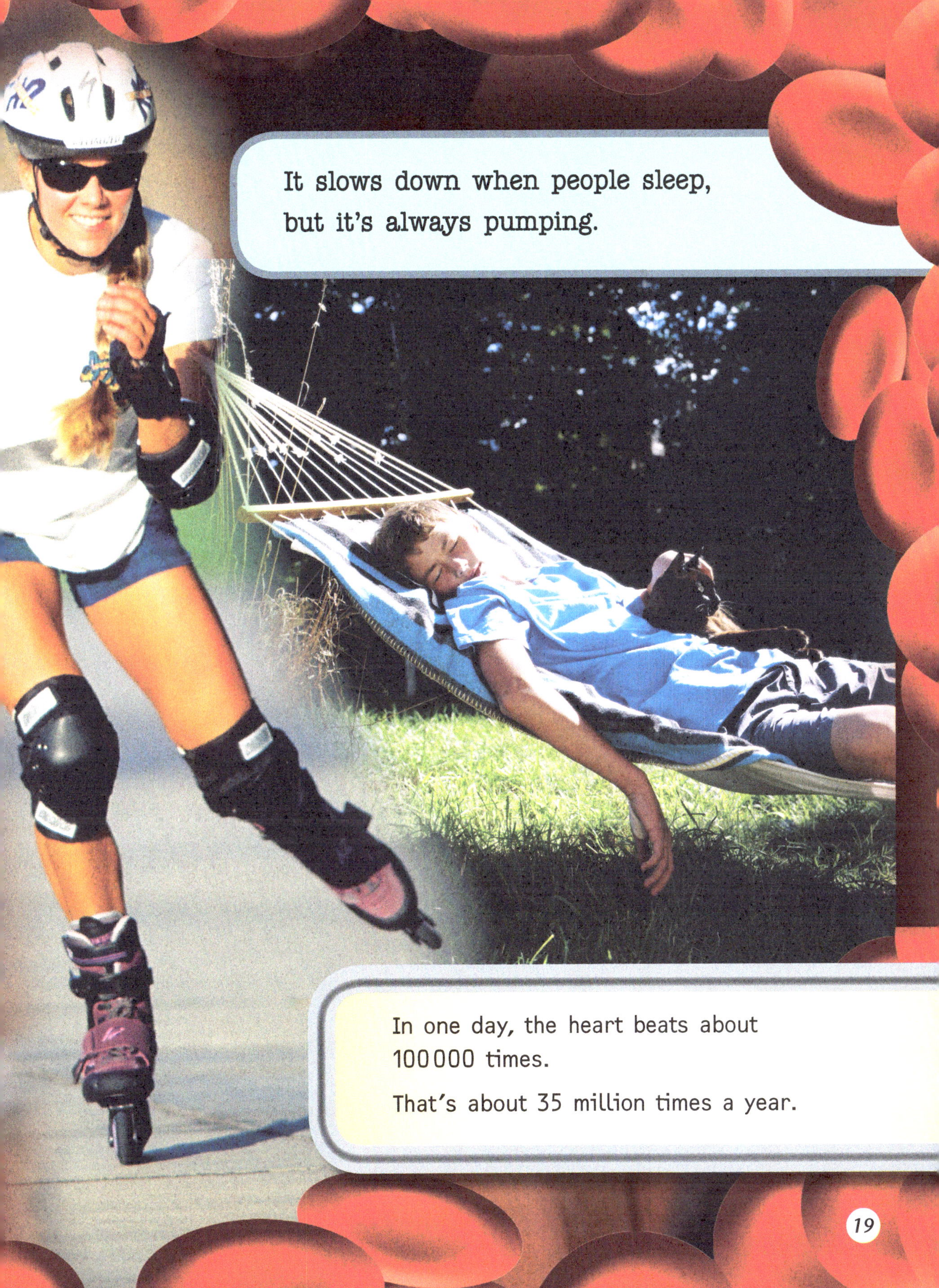

It slows down when people sleep, but it's always pumping.

In one day, the heart beats about 100 000 times.

That's about 35 million times a year.

THE HEALTHY HEART

A healthy heart can pump oxygen-filled blood around the body.

When the heart isn't healthy, the body doesn't work as well as it should.

The way you move and the food you eat has a lot to do with how well your heart works.

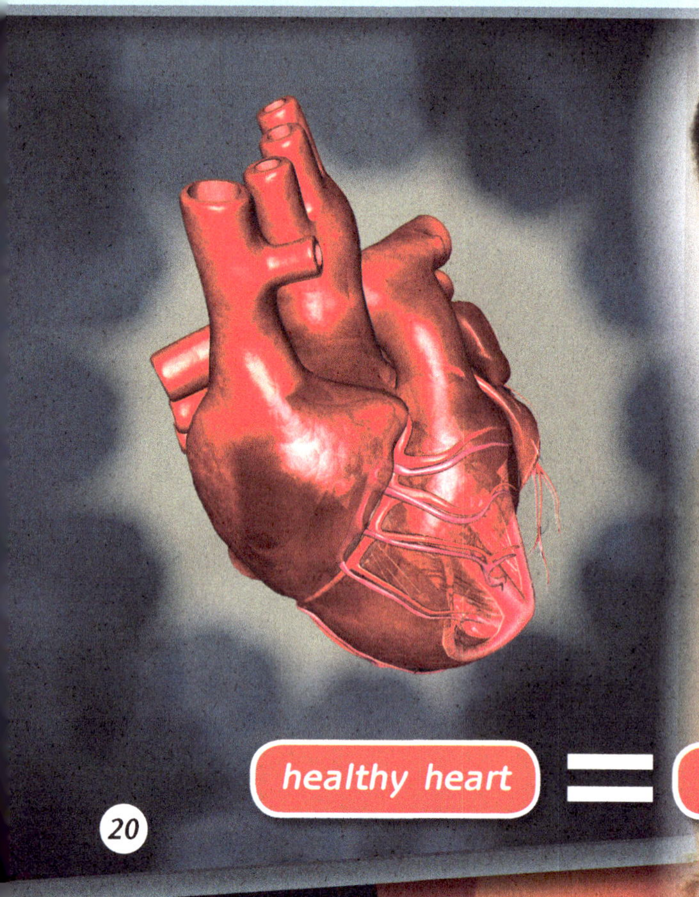

healthy heart = healthy person

Here are three ways to keep the heart healthy:

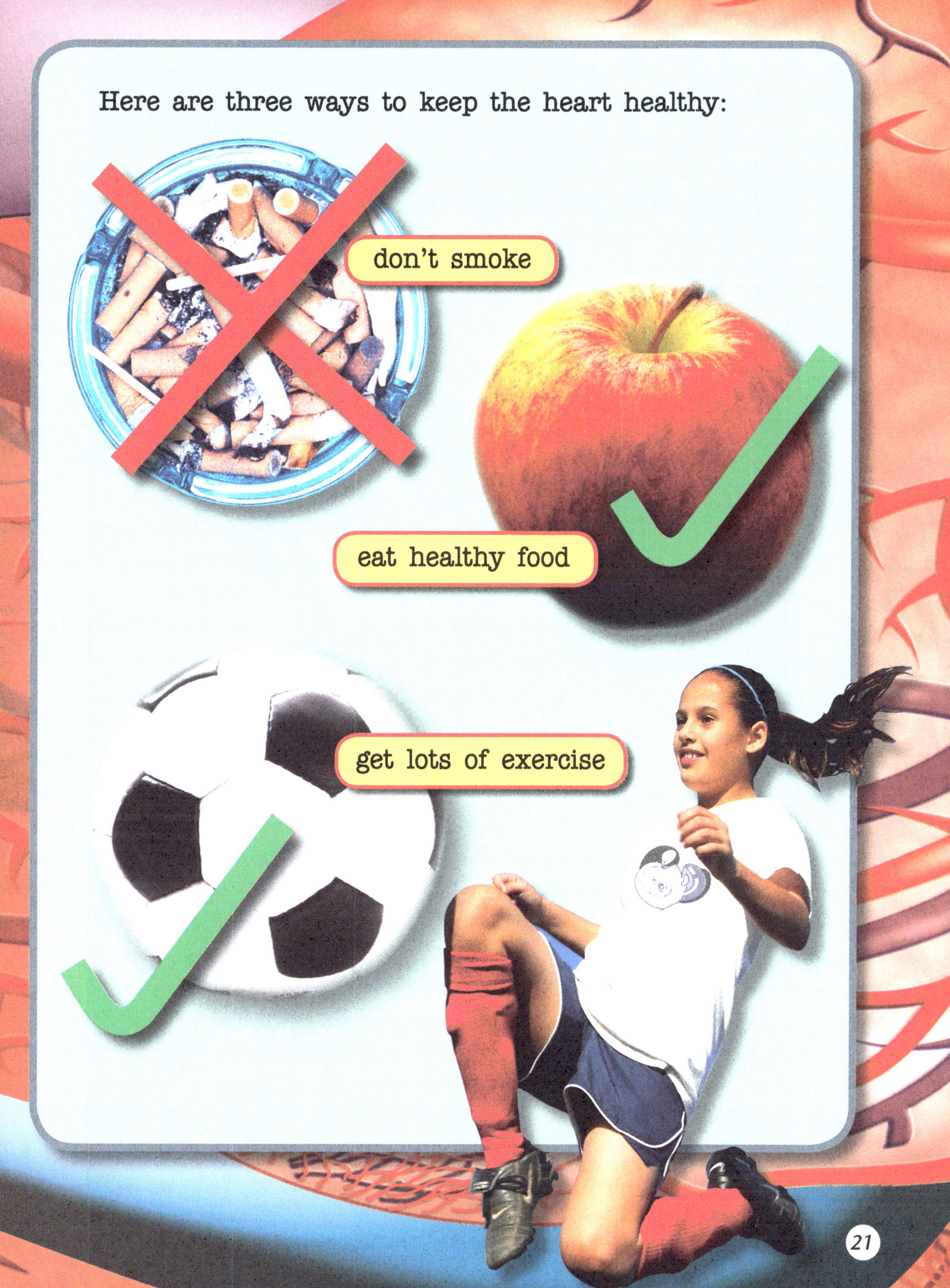

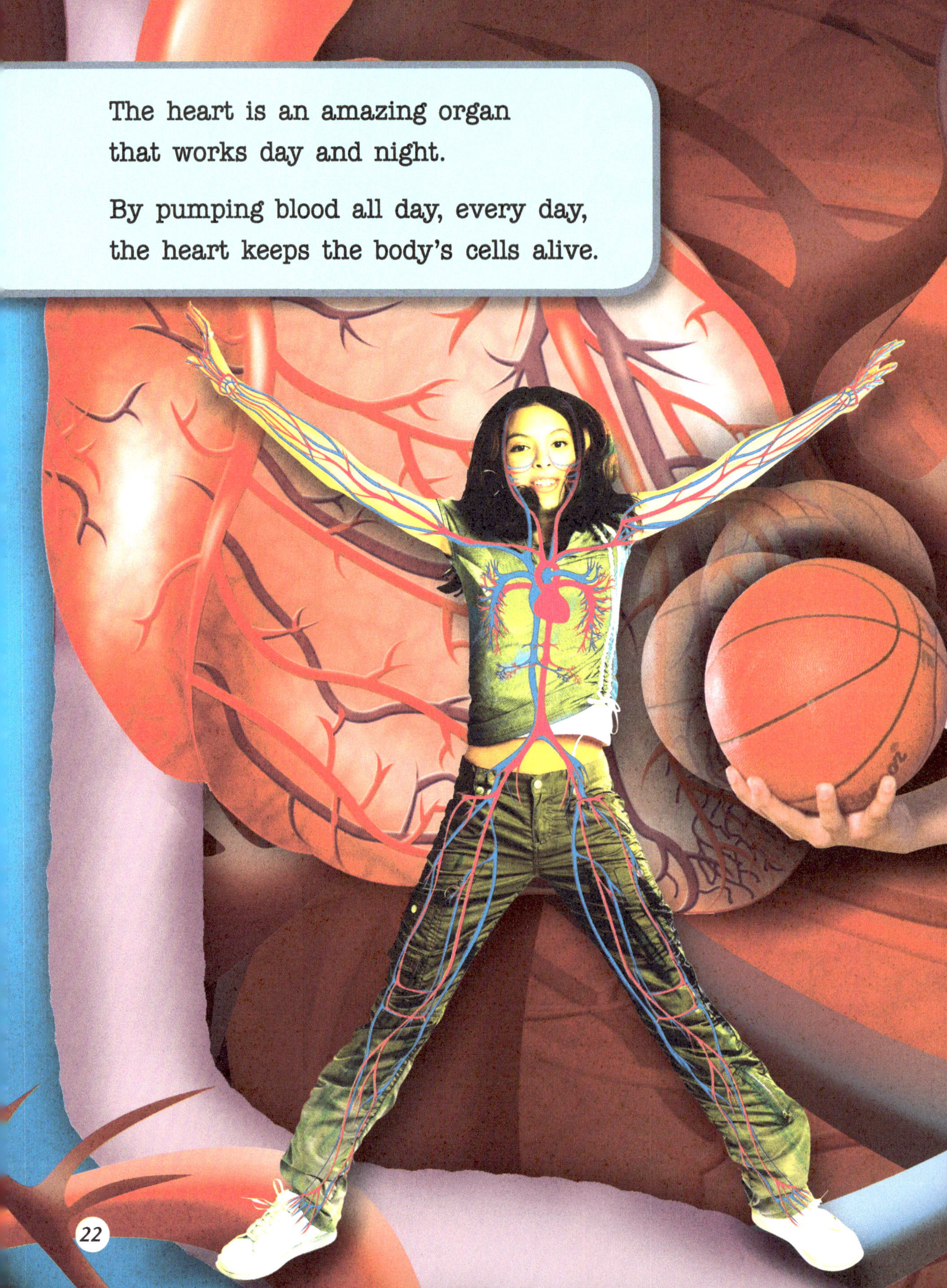

The heart is an amazing organ that works day and night.

By pumping blood all day, every day, the heart keeps the body's cells alive.

In a lifetime, the heart beats about 2.5 billion times.

This is an amazing job for an organ that is only about the size of a fist.

Glossary

cell the smallest structural unit of a living thing

organs parts of the body that perform a specific function. The heart, lungs and brain are all organs.

valves openings in an organ or blood vessel that allow blood to flow through in one direction

Index